To:-
From:-

HELEN EXLEY GIFTBOOKS
thoughtful giving starts here...

OTHER BOOKS IN THE TO-GIVE-AND-TO-KEEP® SERIES:
Wishing you Happiness
To a very special Mother
To someone special in Times of Trouble
To my very special Husband
Wishing you the Best Birthday Ever

Dedication: For <u>my</u> very special friend, Heather Gibbons – a truly
wonderful little person! Lots of love and thousands of thank you's,
from Juliette.

Published simultaneously in 1992 by Helen Exley Giftbooks in Great
Britain, and Helen Exley Giftbooks LLC in the USA.
First published in Great Britain in 1991 by Helen Exley Giftbooks

12   11   10

ISBN 1-86187-350-6

Illustrations Juliette Clarke.
Edited by Helen Exley.
Printed in China.

Helen Exley Giftbooks, 16 Chalk Hill, Watford, Herts WD19 4BG, United Kingdom.
Helen Exley Giftbooks LLC, 185 Main Street, Spencer, MA 01562, USA.
www.helenexleygiftbooks.com

'TO A VERY SPECIAL'® AND 'TO-GIVE-AND-TO-KEEP'®
ARE REGISTERED TRADE MARKS OF EXLEY PUBLICATIONS LTD
AND EXLEY PUBLICATIONS LLC.
PAM BROWN, MARION C. GARRETTY, JUDITH C. GRANT,
MAYA V. PATEL: published with permission © Helen Exley 1992.

BY MY SIDE

Don't walk in front of me,
I may not follow.
Don't walk behind me,
I may not lead.
Walk beside me,
And just be my friend.

AUTHOR UNKNOWN

. . .

My friend. You never expect too much
of me. You are glad when I succeed,
but failure makes no difference to you.
You give me all the help you can - but,
more important, you are simply there.

WENDY JEAN SMITH

. . .

WHAT IS A FRIEND?

A friend is a person with whom you dare to be
yourself.

PAM BROWN, b. 1928

. . .

A friend is someone who dislikes the same people
you dislike.

ANONYMOUS

. . .

. . . A friend doesn't go on a diet because you are fat.
A friend never defends a husband who gets his wife
an electric skillet for her birthday. A friend will tell
you she saw your old boyfriend - and he's a priest.

ERMA BOMBECK (1927-1996)

. . .

Friend derives from a word meaning "free". A friend is
someone who allows us the space and freedom to be.

DEBBIE ALICEN

. . .

Real friends are those who, when you've made
a fool of yourself, don't feel that you've done a
permanent job.

H.M.E.

. . .

THE COMFORT OF SMALL THINGS

Oh, the comfort – the inexpressible comfort, of feeling *safe* with a person – having neither to weigh thoughts nor measure words, but pouring them all right out, just as they are chaff and grain together; certain that a faithful hand will take and sift them, keep what is worth keeping, and then, with the breath of kindness blow the rest away.

DINAH MARIA MULOCK CRAIK (1826-1887)

. . .

And all people live, not by reason of any care they have for themselves, but by the love for them that is in other people.

LEO TOLSTOY (1828 - 1910)

. . .

The happiness of life is made up of minute fractions - the little soon-forgotten charities of a kiss or a smile, a kind look, or heartfelt compliment.

SAMUEL TAYLOR COLERIDGE (1772 - 1834)

. . .

Friends run across the road with a plate of freshly baked scones.

Friends fetch you to see the newly born kittens.

Friends take cuttings for you.

Friends leave bags of apples on the doorstep.

Friends clear the snow off your side of the driveway.

Friends stop the papers when you forgot.

Friends feed the cat.

Friends are absolutely indispensable.

JUDITH C. GRANT, b. 1960

A friend, by a phone call,
a popping-in,
a chance meeting,
a small unexpected
surprise, puts a little jam on
the day's bread and butter.

J.R.C.

A FRIEND IS . . .

A friend knows how to allow for mere quantity in your talk, and only replies to the quality...

WILLIAM DEAN HOWELLS (1837 - 1920)

. . .

Friends stay friends because they don't mess about in each other's lives.

RICHARD ALAN

. . .

A friend respects your diet.

PAM BROWN, b. 1928

. . .

A friend never says "I told you so" - even when she did.

WENDY JEAN SMITH

. . .

NO NEED TO SPEAK

I always felt that the great high privilege, relief and
comfort of friendship was that one had to explain
nothing.

KATHERINE MANSFIELD (1888 - 1923)

. . .

True friendship comes when silence between two
people is comfortable.

DAVE TYSON GENTRY

. . .

Silences make the real conversations between friends. Not the saying but the never needing to say is what counts.

MARGARET LEE RUNBECK

. . .

There was nothing remote or mysterious here - only something private. The only secret was the ancient communication between two people.

EUDORA WELTY (1909-2001)

. . .

A friend hears the song in my heart and sings it to me when my memory fails.

from *"Pioneer Girls Leaders' Handbook"*

. . .

. . . when people have light in themselves, it will shine out from them. Then we get to know each other as we walk together in the darkness, without needing to pass our hands over each other's faces, or to intrude into each other's hearts.

ALBERT SCHWEITZER (1875 - 1965)

. . .

THAT VERY SPECIAL FRIEND

We cannot tell the precise moment when friendship
is formed. As in filling a vessel drop by drop, there
is at last a drop which makes it run over; so in a
series of kindnesses there is at last one which makes
the heart run over.

JAMES BOSWELL (1740 - 1795)

. . .

First of all things, for friendship, there must be that
delightful, indefinable state called feeling at ease
with your companion, the one man, the one woman
out of a multitude who interests you, who meets
your thoughts and tastes.

JULIA DUHRING

. . .

Then little by little we discover one friend, in the midst of the crowd of friends, who is particularly happy to be with us and to whom, we realize, we have an infinite number of things to say. She is not the top of the class, she is not particularly well thought of by the others, she does not wear showy clothes... and when we are walking home with her we realize that her shoes are identical to ours - strong and simple, not showy and flimsy like those of our other friends . . .

NATALIA GINZBURG (1916-1991), from *"The Little Virtues"*

. . .

Friends do not live in harmony merely, as some say, but in melody.

HENRY DAVID THOREAU (1817 - 1862)

. . .

. . . BY BEING YOURSELF

I love you not only for what you are,
but for what I am when I am with you.

I love you not only for what you have made
of yourself, but for what you are making of me.

I love you because you have done more than
any creed could have done to make me good,
and more than any fate could have done to
make me happy.

You have done it without a touch,
without a word, without a sign.

You have done it by being yourself. Perhaps that is
what being a friend means, after all.

ROY CROFT

. . .

Life is nothing without friendship.

CICERO (106 - 43 BC)

. . .

Of all the things which wisdom provides to
make life entirely happy, much the greatest is
the possession of friendship.

EPICURUS (341 - 270 BC)

. . .

Friendship is unnecessary, like philosophy, like
art... It has no survival value; rather it is one of
those things that give value to survival.

C. S. LEWIS (1898 - 1963)

. . .

Friendship improves happiness, and abates
misery, by doubling our joy, and dividing our
grief.

JOSEPH ADDISON (1672 - 1719)

. . .

Love is caviar and wedding cake, strawberries and cream. Love is champagne. Friendship is new bread, fresh butter, farmhouse cheese and a pot of tea for two. Of course, to get through life, it's best to combine the two. But friendship is easier on the digestion.

PAM BROWN, b. 1928

. . .

The truth is friendship is to me every bit as sacred as eternal marriage.

KATHERINE MANSFIELD (1888 - 1923)

. . .

THANK YOU!

If I were to make a solemn speech in praise of you, in gratitude, in deep affection, you would turn an alarming shade of crimson and try to escape. So I won't.

Take it all as said.

MARION C. GARRETTY, b. 1917

. . .

I want just one thing.
To live long enough to pay back in some way your undeserved and overwhelming generosity.

PAM BROWN, b. 1928

. . .

The hardest thing is not to be able to
work magic for a friend.

MAYA V. PATEL, b. 1943

. . .

I no doubt deserved my enemies, but
I don't believe I deserved my friends.

WALT WHITMAN (1819 - 1892)

. . .

As long as there is a post and the telephone is not cut off, so long as we have things to tell and joys and anxieties to share - we will be friends. Always.

MARION C. GARRETTY, b. 1917

. . .

I think there is, in friendship, an instant recognition - a kind of loving. It needs only a word in passing, the touch of a hand - yet parting is loss, and the tiny ache of regret stays with us always.

H.M.E.

. . .

FAR AWAY

In loneliness, in sickness, in confusion - the mere
knowledge of friendship makes it possible to
endure, even if the friend is powerless to help. It is
enough that they exist.
Friendship is not diminished by distance or time, by
imprisonment or war, by suffering or silence. It is in
these things that it roots most deeply. It is from
these things that it flowers.

PAM BROWN, b. 1928

. . .

Here at the frontier, there are falling leaves.
Although my neighbours are all barbarians,
And you, you are a thousand miles away,
There are always two cups on my table.

T'ANG DYNASTY (618 - 906 A.D.)

. . .

There's nothing worth
the wear of winning, but
laughter and the love of
friends.

HILAIRE BELLOC

(1870 - 1953)

. . .

QUOTATIONS ABOUT FRIENDSHIP

God gave us our relatives; thank God we can choose our friends.

ETHEL WATTS MUMFORD (1878 - 1940)

. . .

Treat your friends as you do your pictures, and place them in their best light.

JENNIE JEROME CHURCHILL (1854 - 1921)

. . .

"Stay" is a charming word in a friend's vocabulary.

LOUISA MAY ALCOTT (1832 - 1888)

. . .

The worst solitude is to be destitute of sincere friendship.

FRANCIS BACON (1561 - 1626)

. . .

But every road is rough to me that has no friend to cheer it.

ELIZABETH SHANE fl. 1920s

. . .

A TROUBLE SHARED

It is not so much our friends'
help that helps us as the
confident knowledge that
they will help us.
EPICURUS (341 - 270 BC)

. . .

I never crossed your
threshold with a grief,
but that I went without it.
THEODOSIA GARRISON
(1874 - 1944)

. . .

It is the friends you can call up at 4 a.m. that matter.

MARLENE DIETRICH, (1904-1992)

. . .

A friend is someone who arrives when you have flu
with a bag of oranges, the thriller you wanted to
read and a bunch of flowers. They put the flowers in
a vase, make you a hot drink, do the washing up -
and go.

PAM BROWN, b. 1928

. . .

When a friend asks there is no tomorrow.

GEORGE HERBERT (1593 - 1633)

. . .

A real friend is one who walks in when the rest of
the world walks out.

WALTER WINCHELL (1879 - 1972)

. . .

SHARING

Grief can take care of itself, but to get the full value of a joy you must have somebody to divide it with.

MARK TWAIN (1835 - 1910)

. . .

Happiness seems made to be shared.

JEAN RACINE (1639 - 1699)

. . .

Friends, companions, lovers, are those who treat us in terms of our unlimited worth to ourselves. They are closest to us who best understand what life means to us, who feel for us as we feel for ourselves, who are bound to us in triumph and disaster, who break the spell of our loneliness.

HENRY ALONZO MYERS

. . . It is that my friends have made the story of my life. In a thousand ways they have turned my limitations into beautiful privileges, and enabled me to walk serene and happy in the shadow cast by my deprivation.

HELEN KELLER (1880 - 1968)

. . .

What do we live for, if it is not to make life less difficult for each other?

MARY ANN EVANS (GEORGE ELIOT) (1819 - 1880)

. . .